Just Nicholas

By Annie Kratzsch
Illustrated by Tessa Janes

matthiasmedia
SYDNEY · YOUNGSTOWN

Matthias Media
(St Matthias Press Ltd ACN 067 558 365)
Email: info@matthiasmedia.com.au
Internet: www.matthiasmedia.com.au
Please visit our website for current postal and telephone contact information.

Matthias Media (USA)
Email: sales@matthiasmedia.com
Internet: www.matthiasmedia.com
Please visit our website for current postal and telephone contact information.

ISBN 978 1 922206 79 4

Cover design and typesetting by Lankshear Design.

To our parents, who helped form this dream;
and to our husbands, who helped make it possible.

Nicholas lived long ago in a big white house on a green hill by the blue sea. In the garden behind his house he grew orange flowers and trees with juicy yellow fruit.

On warm afternoons, Nicholas walked in the cool shade of his fruit trees.
In the chilly evenings, he sat in his house by the glowing fireplace.

Nicholas's mother and father had died when he was young,
and he had no wife or children. So no-one else lived in
the white house or enjoyed the beautiful garden.

Just Nicholas.

But Nicholas was not lonely.

Nicholas loved God. Every day he sat on a bench in his beautiful garden and talked to God. He shared his worries. He thanked God for every good thing.

Nicholas also had many friends in the village.

He often walked down the hill to the sea to visit his friend Plutus, who was a fisherman. Nicholas and Plutus enjoyed talking after they pulled nets of colorful fish from Plutus's boat.

One day, Nicholas saw that his friend looked sad. He put his hand on Plutus's shoulder and asked, "What's wrong, Plutus?"

"Oh, Nicholas", Plutus said. "I'm very worried. I am getting old, and I have no money. What will happen to my three daughters when I am too old to look after them any more?"

Tears filled his eyes.

"God knows you're worried, Plutus. But no problem is too big for God. Let's ask him to help you."

"Thank you, Nicholas", Plutus said. "But I think this problem is too big even for God."

"We'll see", said Nicholas. And with a wink, he waved goodbye.

As he walked, Nicholas talked to God.

"God, my friend Plutus is in trouble", he said. "Please help him. And please show me how I can help."

When he arrived home, Nicholas looked around. He knew that everything he had was a gift from God.

He had clothes to wear and food to eat. He had beautiful paintings on the walls and soft carpets on the floors. He had gold coins to buy whatever he needed.

But Nicholas knew that his greatest treasure was one that couldn't be seen.

When Nicholas was a little boy, his mother and father had taught him about God.

"The Bible is God's special book," his mother began, "and it tells us that God made the whole world. It was beautiful and perfect. But then people started saying 'No' to God. They did what they wanted instead of what God told them to do. This is called 'sin'. Sin hurts other people and makes God angry."

"Does God punish people for sin?" Nicholas asked.

His father placed a warm hand on Nicholas's head. "Yes, he does, Nicholas. But the good news is that many years ago God sent his son, Jesus, to help us. Jesus always did what God wanted; he never sinned. But he was killed on a cross."

"He didn't deserve to be punished," Nicholas's mother said quietly, "but he took *our* punishment for us. And that means we can be friends with God again."

"Why did Jesus do that?" Nicholas asked.

"Because he loves us so much", his father explained.

At first Nicholas was happy, but then he began to cry.

"What's wrong, Nicholas?" His mother squeezed him tightly.

"I'm so sad that Jesus is dead", Nicholas said.

His father smiled a wide, bright smile. "Oh, no, Nicholas",
he said. "That's the best news of all. Jesus died, but God made him
alive again! And he lives with God forever."

"What should I give Jesus for doing this for me?" Nicholas asked.

"What Jesus did for you is free. It is the best gift you can ever receive",
his father said. "You don't need to give him anything. But when you
love God, and when you understand how much he has loved you,
you'll want to share God's love with others."

Grown-up Nicholas stood by his fireplace in the room where his
mother and father had told him this special and true story.
It made him happy to think of his parents and to
remember all they had taught him.

He prayed for his friend Plutus and his big problem.
He thought about Jesus's greatest gift.

Suddenly, he had an idea.

That night, the air grew cold and snow began to fall. The green
hill turned silver in the moonlight. The sea was purple under the dark sky.

Nicholas put on his red cloak and pulled up the hood.

He was so thankful for what God had given him that he wanted to share what
he had with other people. But he wanted to give his gifts in secret.

Nicholas tiptoed down the hill into the sleeping town.
Something jingled softly in his pocket.

Plutus's house was dark. Nicholas could hear Plutus snoring behind the closed windows and doors. He walked around the outside of the house but couldn't find anywhere to leave his gifts.

Finally, he spotted a small opening in one window, just big enough for his hand to slip through.

Nicholas looked this way. He looked that way. He couldn't see anyone.

He took three small bags from his pocket and tossed them into the house.

One! Two! Three! Chink! Chink! Chink! They landed right in front of the fireplace.

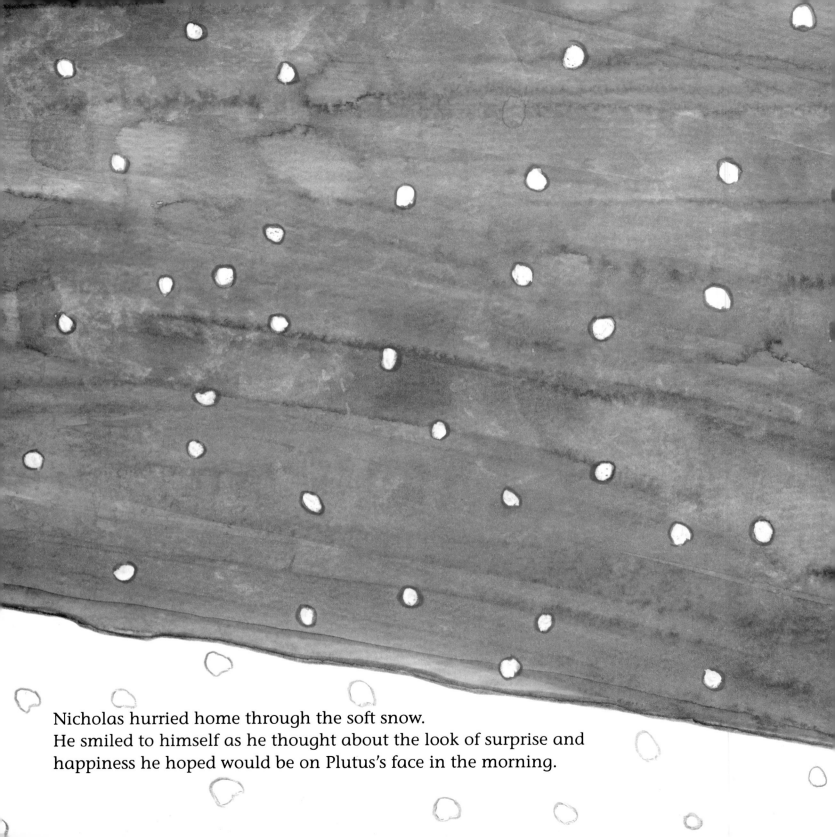

Nicholas hurried home through the soft snow.
He smiled to himself as he thought about the look of surprise and
happiness he hoped would be on Plutus's face in the morning.

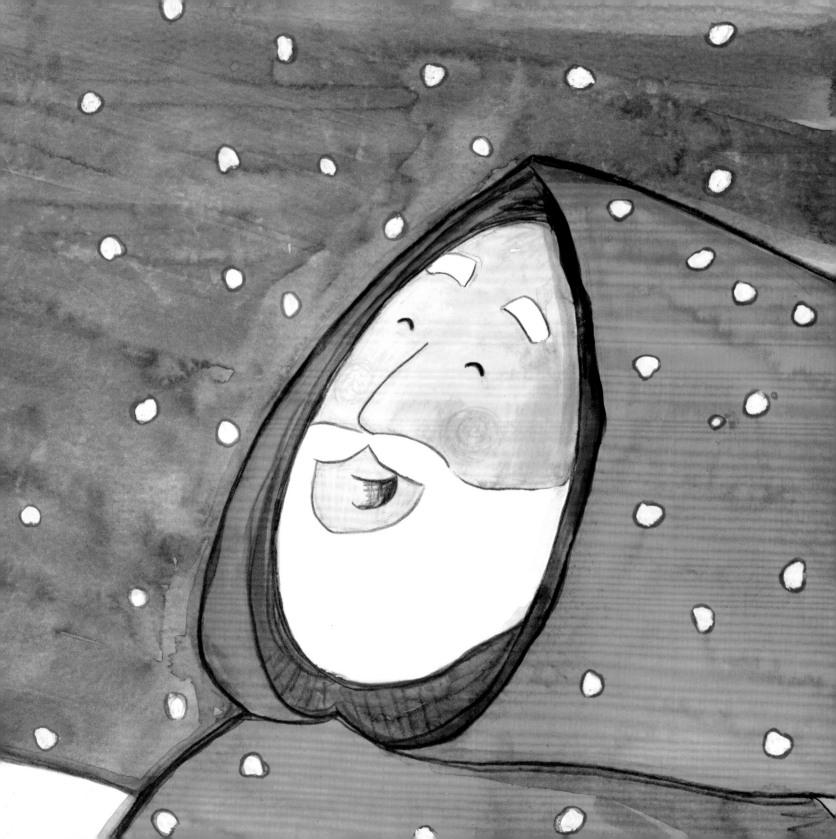

The next morning, Nicholas found Plutus down by the sea. His friend looked happy.

"Nicholas!" Plutus said. "God has done an amazing thing for me and my daughters! Yesterday, you said I should ask God for help. I didn't really believe he would help me, but this morning I found three bags of gold by the fireplace, right beside my shoes. Each bag was filled with more than enough money to care for my daughters. Isn't it wonderful?"

"That *is* wonderful! Thank you, God!" Nicholas said, and he hugged his friend.

"How do you think God did this?" Plutus asked.

"God gives gifts in lots of different ways", Nicholas said. "The important thing is to thank him."

From that day on, Nicholas shared everything God had given him with anyone who needed it.

He gave to the sick.
He gave to the poor.
He gave to the lonely.
He gave to friends and strangers.

And he always gave in secret. He wanted people to remember that everything we have comes from God. He wanted people to give their thanks to God.

As his big white house emptied, his heart filled with love and thankfulness to God.

Even though he gave his gifts in secret, stories soon spread about Nicholas. People saw that he loved God, so they gave him a special name: Saint Nicholas.

On one cold night every December, parents would tell their children the story of Nicholas. The children heard about Nicholas's generous gifts and how much he loved Jesus. When they went to bed, they left their shoes near the fireplace or near a door or window.

While the children slept, their parents filled the shoes with treats to find in the morning. They called this Saint Nicholas Day.

Many people also thought of Saint Nicholas at Christmas time, when they gave gifts to each other to remember God's greatest gift of all: the birth of the baby Jesus.

Over the years, people imagined stories about Nicholas—exciting, magical and sometimes silly stories. Some people gave him nicknames, like Saint Nick, Father Christmas, Kris Kringle, or Santa Claus, and they started to forget the true story about the real person called Nicholas.

At Christmas, when you celebrate
Jesus's birthday and open your presents,
remember the true story of Jesus, God's greatest gift,
who died for you so that you can be friends with God.

And when you see pictures of Santa and reindeer and elves,
remember the true story of Nicholas. Nicholas was so thankful
for what God had given him that he gave what he had to help others.

He didn't have magical powers. He was a real person.

He was just Nicholas.

 **TO PARENTS**

Our aim is for this book to serve as a child-friendly voice of truth in the midst of a Santa-saturated Christmas experience.

Here are some questions to explore with your children as you read *Just Nicholas* and make it part of your Christmas tradition.

Is this story really true?

Although the author and illustrator have used their creativity to bring new life to specific sensory details, and the exact chronology and conversations are imagined, all of the events in the story are based in historical texts.

Does that mean Nicholas was a real person?

It does! Nicholas was born in the late third century in what is now Turkey. He was wealthy and his parents died when he was very young. He became a well-known Christian leader in Myra, a coastal town, in the fourth century. People knew and remembered Nicholas for his generous care of those in need.

Was there a real man named Plutus who had three daughters?

The tale of the three daughters, though considered legend by some, has more historical credibility than any other story told about Nicholas. In the story, Nicholas's generous gifts to the daughters also reflect the early Christian church's revolutionary care and concern for women in a culture that traditionally treated them as inferior. Although the real name of the girls' father is unknown, the name Plutus would have been a fairly common one in the region, which was under Greek rule and influence during Nicholas's time.

What is Saint Nicholas Day?

Depending on the country, Saint Nicholas Day is celebrated on either December 6th or 19th, the anniversary of the death of Nicholas of Myra. This holiday celebrates the life of Nicholas by reenacting the story of the three daughters. Children around the world put out their empty shoes the night before Saint Nicholas Day, and parents fill the shoes with special treats for the children to discover in the morning.

Are there other ways in which families can celebrate Saint Nicholas Day?

When you are celebrating a man who gave generously and selflessly, the possibilities are endless! For example:

- Write and send someone a kind note.
- Leave a treat at your neighbor's door.
- Choose a toy to share with or give to someone else.
- Save or raise money to give to an organization that helps people when they need it, either in your local area or internationally, such as Samaritan's Purse (www.samaritanspurse.org) or the Advent Conspiracy (www.adventconspiracy.org).

Does this mean that Nicholas became Santa Claus?

Yes and no. Santa Claus is a character and not a real person. The story of Santa Claus is a legend, or a story that began with an actual event and then evolved into a myth or fictional account. In this case, the actual event was the life of Nicholas.

There are some important differences between Nicholas and Santa Claus. Nicholas gave to people out of love for God and others. He gave sacrificially from his own possessions to meet the needs of those around him. The stories we tell about Santa Claus say that he gives only to those who are 'good' or 'nice', and that his gifts are magically created every year. The story of Nicholas reminds us that God gives based not on what we deserve but on his overflowing love for us.

Is the story Nicholas learned from his parents true?

Absolutely! The original story is found in the Bible, in the four Gospels by Matthew, Mark, Luke and John. These are shorter books within the Bible that give an account of Jesus's life on earth. There are also many wonderful illustrated books that retell this story for children. For toddlers and preschoolers, *Read Aloud Bible Stories* by Ella K Lindvall and H Kent Puckett and *The Beginner's Bible* by Kelly Pulley are simple and delightful. For older children, check out *The Jesus Storybook Bible* by Sally Lloyd-Jones, *The Gospel Story Bible* by Martin Machowski, and *The Big Picture Story Bible* by David Helm.

How and when should parents teach their children the truth about Santa?

There is no 'right' answer to this question. *Just Nicholas* gives parents the opportunity to tell children the truth about Santa Claus from the very beginning, without condemning popular culture or spoiling the 'magic' of Christmas.